P
Ps

MEDITATIONS ON THE PSALMS

Psalms 112-150 taken from the New International Version
Comment by E M Blaiklock Photographs by Gordon Gray

SCRIPTURE UNION

Published by
SCRIPTURE UNION
47 Marylebone Lane London W1M 6AX

ISBN 0 85421 834 3

Books in this series
Book 1 Psalms 1-37
Book 2 Psalms 38-75
Book 3 Psalms 76-111
Book 4 Psalms 112-150

Designed by Tony Cantale

Printed in England by W.S. Cowell Ltd,
Buttermarket, Ipswich.

Book 1 ISBN 0 85421 798 3

Book 2 ISBN 0 85421 832 7

Book 3 ISBN 0 85421 833 5

Book 4 ISBN 0 85421 834 3

112 THE RIGHTEOUS MAN

Praise the LORD.

Blessed is the man who fears the LORD,
who finds great delight in his commands.

²His children will be mighty in the land;
each generation of the upright will be blessed.
³Wealth and riches are in his house,
and his righteousness endures for ever.
⁴Even in darkness light dawns for the upright,
for the gracious and compassionate and righteous man.
⁵Good will come to him who is generous and lends freely,
who conducts his affairs with justice.
⁶Surely he will never be shaken;
a righteous man will be remembered for ever.
⁷He will have no fear of bad news;
his heart is steadfast, trusting in the LORD.
⁸His heart is secure, he will have no fear;
in the end he will look in triumph on his foes.
⁹He has scattered abroad his gifts to the poor,
his righteousness endures for ever;
his horn will be lifted high in honour.

¹⁰The wicked man will see and be vexed,
he will gnash his teeth and waste away;
the longings of the wicked will come to nothing.

This poem picks up the theme of Psalm 111, awe: 'Blessed is the man who fears the Lord' (1). It is the key to the maintenance of the restored people's new-found life (2). A godly fear of evil makes good men, and good men make a good nation.

In a sick society, diseased by violence, righteous men are needed to lighten a growing gloom (4). Grace, compassion (4), generosity, justice (5) can come only from those who are stable, and such are the good (6). The world needs valiant, fearless men (7). If some vast revival could flood the world with such men, the maladies of society would vanish, to the discomfiture of the wicked on whom no pity need be wasted.

113 PRAISE THE LORD

Praise the LORD.

Praise, O servants of the LORD,
praise the name of the LORD.
2 Let the name of the LORD be praised,
both now and for evermore.
3 From the rising of the sun to the place
where it sets
the name of the LORD is to be praised.

4 The LORD is exalted over all the nations,
his glory above the heavens.
5 Who is like the LORD our God,
the One who sits enthroned on high,
6 who stoops down to look
on the heavens and the earth?

7 He raises the poor from the dust
and lifts the needy from the ash heap;
8 he seats them with princes,
with the princes of their people.
9 He settles the barren woman in her home
as a happy mother of children.

Praise the LORD.

This is the first of the psalms comprising the Hallel, sung at the Passover, Pentecost and the Feast of Tents. The sequence of six, opening, it was said, with a psalm of Moses, was called, from Psalm 114.1, the 'Egyptian Hallel'. This psalm and the next were sung before the Passover meal, and Psalms 115 to 118 at its conclusion. Hence the hymn after the last supper.

'The name of the Lord', meant the Lord and all he signified (1, 2, 3). Praise is awe or reverence, an attitude rather than words. That is how it is possible to 'pray continually' (1 Thessalonians 5.17). Verse 6 seems to glimpse the Incarnation from afar (Philippians 2.8). In her prayer of thanks (1 Samuel 2.8), Hannah used the words of verses 7 and 8, an indication of how very old was at least part of this prayer. The 'poor and needy' are all of us, as Andrew Carnegie said as he lay dying.

114 THE EARTH TREMBLES

When Israel came out of Egypt,
the house of Jacob from a people of foreign tongue,
2 Judah became God's sanctuary,
Israel his dominion.
3 The sea looked and fled,
the Jordan turned back;
4 the mountains skipped like rams,
the hills like lambs.

5 Why was it, O sea, that you fled,
O Jordan, that you turned back,
6 you mountains, that you skipped like rams,
you hills, like lambs?

7 Tremble, O earth, at the presence of the Lord,
at the presence of the God of Jacob,
8 who turned the rock into a pool,
the hard rock into springs of water.

The people of the Restoration thought much about the Exodus. It was like a repetition of history. Indeed, when has: 'Let my people go', not been a demand of that harassed and scattered race? Today's news must be read in the light of it.

Nature itself seemed to facilitate their marching, the walls of the waves opening before them . . . Perhaps verse 4 refers to tremors of the land which dammed the Jordan, as it has been dammed on three other recorded occasions, to allow the passage of the Israelites. The inanimate earth obeyed its Lord, gave and withheld as he decreed. How much more should animate creation 'praise his name'!

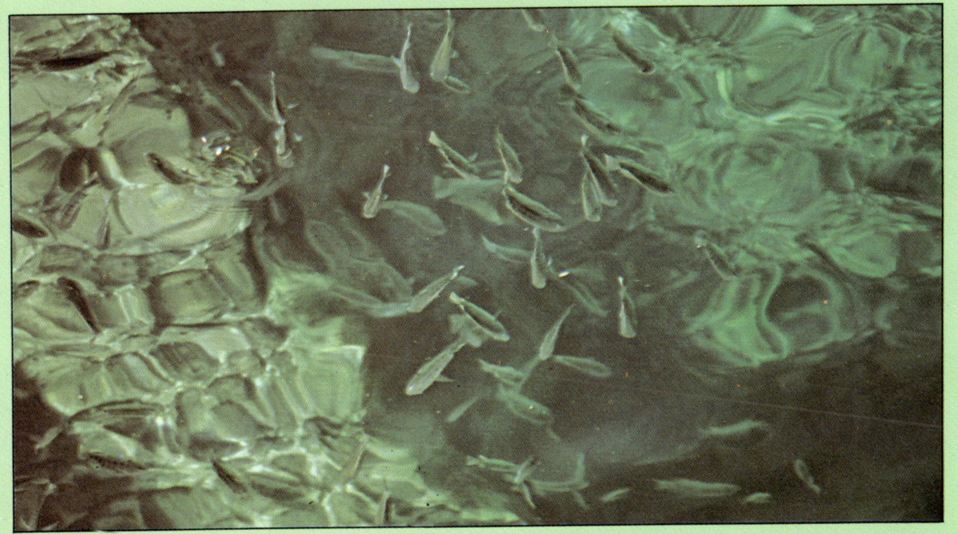

115 HE WILL BLESS

Not to us, O LORD, not to us
but to your name be the glory,
because of your love and faithfulness.

2Why do the nations say,
'Where is their God?'
3Our God is in heaven;
he does whatever pleases him.
4But their idols are silver and gold,
made by the hands of men.
5They have mouths, but cannot speak,
eyes, but they cannot see;
6they have ears, but cannot hear,
noses, but they cannot smell;
7they have hands, but cannot feel,
feet, but they cannot walk;
nor can they utter a sound with their
throats.
8Those who make them will be like them,
and so will all who trust in them.

9O house of Israel, trust in the LORD –
he is their help and shield.
10O house of Aaron, trust in the LORD –
he is their help and shield.
11You who tear him, trust in the LORD –
he is their help and shield.

12The LORD remembers us and will bless
us:
he will bless the house of Israel,
he will bless the house of Aaron,
13he will bless those who fear the LORD –
small and great alike.

14May the LORD make you increase,
both you and your children.

15May you be blessed by the LORD,
the Maker of heaven and earth.

[16]The highest heavens belong to the LORD,
but the earth he has given to man.
[17]It is not the dead who praise the LORD,
those who go down to silence;
[18]it is we who extol the LORD,
both now and for evermore.

Praise the LORD.

Perhaps the earlier days of the Restoration lie behind this hymn. Far away in exile, the heathen had scoffed at the unseen Hebrew God, they who, in such obvious absurdity, made deities with their hands, things as helpless and insensate as their foolish makers (8).

The Jew thought with utter contempt of idols. Speaking on the rocky hillock where the philosophers' court met, Paul could see the Acropolis of Athens, with the lovely Parthenon, and the statue of Athene Promachos. He dismissed such awesome art with a sweep of the hand. It was nonsense to a Jew (Acts 17.16, 24-30).

One can almost trace the act of worship, the congregation singing in unison (1-11), the solo words of the Levite choir-leader (12-15) at the time of the actual sacrifice, and then the closing of the service (16-18).

116 DELIVERANCE

I love the LORD, for he heard my
voice;
he heard my cry for mercy.
2Because he turned his ear to me,
I will call on him as long as I live.

3The cords of death entangled me,
the anguish of the grave came upon me;
I was overcome by trouble and sorrow.
4Then I called on the name of the LORD:
'O LORD, save me!'

5The LORD is gracious and righteous;
our God is full of compassion.
6The LORD protects the simple-hearted;
when I was in great need, he saved me.

7Be at rest once more, O my soul,
for the LORD has been good to you.
8For you, O LORD, have delivered my soul
from death,
my eyes from tears,
my feet from stumbling,
9that I may walk before the LORD
in the land of the living.
10I believed; therefore I said,
'I am greatly afflicted.'
11And in my dismay I said,
'All men are liars.'

12How can I repay the LORD
for all his goodness to me?
13I will lift up the cup of salvation
and call on the name of the LORD.
14I will fulfil my vows to the LORD
in the presence of his people.

15Precious in the sight of the LORD
is the death of his saints.

[16]O LORD, truly I am your servant;
I am your servant, the son of your maidservant;
you have freed me from my chains.

[17]I will sacrifice a thank-offering to you
and call on the name of the LORD.
[18]I will fulfil my vows to the LORD
in the presence of all his people,
[19]in the courts of the house of the LORD –
in your midst, O Jerusalem.

Praise the LORD.

This intensely moving little prayer looks like a psalm of David, but no guiding hint is given. Perhaps the compiler, gathering the small collections of psalms which formed his fifth book, placed here a hymn of personal thanksgiving for the passing of illness or trouble, which had intruded on his work. Danger, whatever it was, has been real (3, 8, 15). How touching and universal is verse 8. It is a psalm for any one of us, as Augustine commented: 'Let the soul which wanders from the Lord sing this; let the son who was dead and has come back to life sing this . . . let our souls sing this, brothers . . .' Verses 3 and 4 echo Psalm 18.1-6 showing how real were the ancient words in the minds and hearts of the exiles. The high days of Scottish Christianity knew this same benediction. There was no help, the suppliant found, as thousands since Job have found, in men: 'All men are liars' (11). 'Bury your sorrow', as the old hymn had it——but tell it to God (13). The Psalmist found salvation there, healing and a new zest for life (17-19).

117 GREAT IS HIS LOVE

Praise the LORD, all you nations;
extol him, all you peoples.
2 For great is his love towards us
and the faithfulness of the LORD endures
for ever.

Praise the LORD.

This tiny psalm is not a fragment. The exiled compiler (as we have imagined him) found it, a piece apart and placed it here among his 'Hallel' psalms. Paul quoted the first verse (Romans 15.11) along with words of similar intent from Deuteronomy and Isaiah, to indicate from the scriptures that the Gentiles, too, had their part in the plan of God.

118 THE CAPSTONE

Give thanks to the LORD for he is good;
his love endures for ever.

2 Let Israel say:
'His love endures for ever.'
3 Let the house of Aaron say:
'His love endures for ever.'
4 Let those who fear the LORD say:
'His love endures for ever.'

5 In my anguish I cried to the LORD,
and he answered by setting me free.
6 The LORD is with me; I will not be afraid.
What can man do to me?
7 The LORD is with me; he is my helper.
I will look in triumph on my enemies.
8 It is better to take refuge in the LORD
than to trust in man.
9 It is better to take refuge in the LORD
that to trust in princes.

10 All the nations surrounded me,
but in the name of the LORD I cut them off.
11 They surrounded me on every side,
but in the name of the LORD I cut them off.
12 They swarmed around me like bees,
but they died out as quickly as burning thorns;
in the name of the LORD I cut them off.

13 I was pushed back and about to fall,
but the LORD helped me.
14 The LORD is my strength and my song;
he has become my salvation.

15 Shouts of joy and victory
resound in the tents of the righteous:
'The LORD'S right hand has done mighty things!
16 The LORD'S right hand is lifted high;
the LORD'S right hand has done mighty things!'

17 I will not die but live,
and will proclaim what the LORD has done.
18 The LORD has chastened me severely,
but he has not given me over to death.
19 Open for me the gates of righteousness;
I will enter and give thanks to the LORD.
20 This is the gate of the LORD
through which the righteous may enter.
21 I will give thanks, for you answered me;
you have become my salvation.

22 The stone the builders rejected
has become the capstone;
23 the LORD has done this,
and it is marvellous in our eyes.
24 This is the day the LORD has made;
let us rejoice and be glad in it.

25 O LORD, save us;
O LORD, grant us success.
26 Blessed is he who comes in the name of the LORD.
From the house of the LORD we bless you.
27 The LORD is God,
and he has made his light shine upon us.
With boughs in hand, join in the festal procession
up to the horns of the altar.

28 You are my God, and I will give you thanks;
you are my God, and I will exalt you.

29 Give thanks to the LORD, for he is good;
his love endures for ever.

This festival hymn would fit admirably the mood in Jerusalem when the heroic efforts of Nehemiah were building successfully the defensive walls. Enemies were all around. The Persian king was clearly unable to hold firm control over armed governors in distant provinces, and Nehemiah, for all the royal authority which had made him satrap of Judea, was forced to build with sword in hand (Nehemiah 4.17, 23). Read the psalm in the light of Nehemiah's fourth chapter, and see the words fall into place.

Some actual incident must have given rise to this saying (22)—a rejected stone became an important corner-lock and was seen as a fine symbol of history (22). It signified the Restoration, and was taken up by the Lord, Peter, and Paul (Matthew 21. 42-44; Acts 4.11; 1 Peter 2.7; Ephesians 2.20). The restored Jews had linked the incident (if this guess is justified) with a word of Isaiah (Isaiah 28.16). Israel, consummated in Israel's Messiah, has been a corner-stone of two millenia of history.

119 GOD'S LAW

Blessed are they whose ways are blameless,
who walk according to the law of the LORD.
2 Blessed are they who keep his statutes
and seek him with all their heart.
3 They do nothing wrong;
they walk in his ways.
4 You have laid down precepts
that are to be fully obeyed.
5 Oh, that my ways were steadfast
in obeying your decrees!
6 Then I would not be put to shame
when I consider all your commands.
7 I will praise you with an upright heart
as I learn your righteous laws.
8 I will obey your decrees;
do not utterly forsake me.

9 How can a young man keep his way pure?
By living according to your word.
10 I seek you with all my heart;
do not let me stray from your commands.
11 I have hidden your word in my heart
that I might not sin against you.
12 Praise be to you, O LORD;
teach me your decrees.
13 With my lips I recount
all the laws that come from your mouth.
14 I rejoice in following your statutes
as one rejoices in great riches.
15 I meditate on your precepts
and consider your ways.
16 I delight in your decrees;
I will not neglect your word.

17 Do good to your servant, and I will live;
I will obey your word.
18 Open my eyes that I may see
wonderful things in your law.
19 I am a stranger on earth;
do not hide your commands from me.
20 My soul is consumed with longing
for your laws at all times.
21 You rebuke the arrogant, who are cursed
and who stray from your commands.
22 Remove from me scorn and contempt,
for I keep your statutes.
23 Though princes sit together and slander me,
your servant will meditate on your decrees.
24 Your statutes are my delight;
they are my counsellors.
25 I am laid low in the dust;
renew my life according to your word.
26 I recounted my ways and you answered me;
teach me your decrees.
27 Let me understand the teaching of your precepts;
then I will meditate on your wonders.
28 My soul is weary with sorrow;
strengthen me according to your word.
29 Keep me from deceitful ways;
be gracious to me through your law.
30 I have chosen the way of truth;
I have set my heart on your laws.
31 I hold fast to your statutes, O LORD;
do not let me be put to shame.
32 I run in the path of your commands,
for you have set my heart free.

33 Teach me, O LORD, to follow your decrees;
then I will keep them to the end.
34 Give me understanding, and I will keep your law
and obey it with all my heart.
35 Direct me in the path of your commands,
for there I find delight.
36 Turn my heart towards your statutes
and not towards selfish gain.
37 Turn my eyes away from worthless things;
renew my life according to your word.
38 Fulfil your promise to your servant,
so that you may be feared.
39 Take away the disgrace I dread,
for your laws are good.
40 How I long for your precepts!
Renew my life in your righteousness.

41 May your unfailing love come to me, O LORD,
your salvation according to your promise;
42 then I will answer the one who taunts me,
for I trust in your word.
43 Do not snatch the word of truth from my mouth,
for I have put my hope in your laws.
44 I will always obey your law,
for ever and ever.
45 I will walk about in freedom,
for I have sought out your precepts.
46 I will speak of your statutes before kings
and will not be put to shame,
47 for I delight in your commandments
because I love them.
48 I reach out my hands for your commandments, which I love,
and I meditate on your decrees.
49 Remember your word to your servant,
for you have given me hope.
50 My comfort in my suffering is this:
Your promise renews my life.
51 The arrogant mock me without restraint,
but I do not turn from your law.
52 I remember your ancient laws, O LORD,
and I find comfort in them.

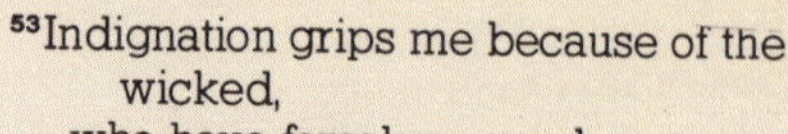

53 Indignation grips me because of the wicked,
who have forsaken your law.
54 Your decrees are the theme of my song
wherever I lodge.
55 In the night I remember your name, O LORD,
and I will keep your law.
56 This has been my practice:
I obey your precepts.

57 You are my portion, O LORD;
I have promised to obey your words.
58 I have sought your face with all my heart;
be gracious to me according to your promise.
59 I have considered my ways
and have turned my steps to your statutes.
60 I will hasten and not delay
to obey your commands.
61 Though the wicked bind me with ropes,
I will not forget your law.
62 At midnight I rise to give you thanks
for your righteous laws.
63 I am a friend to all who fear you,
to all who follow your precepts.
64 The earth is filled with your love O LORD;
teach me your decrees.

65 Do good to your servant
according to your word, O LORD.
66 Teach me knowledge and good judgment,
for I believe in your commands.
67 Before I was afflicted I went astray,
but now I obey your word.
68 You are good, and what you do is good;
teach me your decrees.
69 Though the arrogant have smeared me with lies,
I keep your precepts with all my heart.
70 Their hearts are callous and unfeeling,
but I delight in your law.
71 It was good for me to be afflicted
so that I might learn your decrees.
72 The law from your mouth is more precious to me
than thousands of pieces of silver and gold.

[73]Your hands made me and formed me;
give me understanding to learn your commands.
[74]May they who fear you rejoice when they see me,
for I have put my hope in your word.
[75]I know, O LORD, that your laws are righteous,
and in faithfulness you have afflicted me.
[76]May your unfailing love be my comfort,
according to your promise to your servant.
[77]Let your compassion come to me that I may live,
for your law is my delight.
[78]May the arrogant be put to shame for wronging me without cause;
but I will meditate on your precepts.
[79]May those who fear you turn to me,
those who understand your statutes.
[80]May my heart be blameless towards your decrees,
that I may not be put to shame.

[81]My soul faints with longing for your salvation,
but I have put my hope in your word.
[82]My eyes fail, looking for your promise;
I say, 'When will you comfort me?'
[83]Though I am like a wineskin in the smoke,
I do not forget your decrees.
[84]How long must your servant wait?
When will you punish my persecutors?
[85]The arrogant dig pitfalls for me,
contrary to your law.
[86]All your commands are trustworthy;
help me, for men persecute me without cause.
[87]They almost wiped me from the earth,
but I have not forsaken your precepts.
[88]Preserve my life according to your love,
and I will obey the statutes of your mouth.
[89]Your word, O LORD, is eternal;
it stands firm in the heavens.
[90]Your faithfulness continues through all generations;
you established the earth,
and it endures.
[91]Your laws endure to this day,
for all things serve you.
[92]If your law had not been my delight,
I would have perished in my affliction.
[93]I will never forget your precepts,
for by them you have renewed my life.
[94]Save me, for I am yours;
I have sought out your precepts.

95The wicked are waiting to destroy me,
but I will ponder your statutes.
96To all perfection I see a limit;
but your commands are boundless.

97Oh, how I love your law!
I meditate on it all day long.
98Your commands make me wiser than my enemies,
for they are ever with me.
99I have more insight than all my teachers,
for I meditate on your statutes.
100I have more understanding than the elders,
for I obey your precepts.
101I have kept my feet from every evil path
so that I might obey your word.
102I have not departed from your laws,
for you yourself have taught me.
103How sweet are your promises to my taste,
sweeter than honey to my mouth!
104I gain understanding from your precepts;
therefore I hate every wrong path.

105Your word is a lamp to my feet
and a light for my path.
106I have taken an oath and confirmed it,
that I will follow your righteous laws.
107I have suffered much;
renew my life, O LORD, according to your word.
108Accept, O LORD, the willing praise of my mouth,
and teach me your laws.
109Though I constantly take my life in my hands,
I will not forget your law.
110The wicked have set a snare for me,
but I have not strayed from your precepts.
111Your statutes are my heritage for ever;
they are the joy of my heart.
112My heart is set on keeping your decrees
to the very end.

113I hate double-minded men,
but I love your law.
114You are my refuge and my shield;
I have put my hope in your word.
115Away from me you evildoers,
that I may keep the commands of my God!
116Sustain me according to your promise,
and I shall live;
do not let my hopes be dashed.
117Uphold me, and I shall be delivered;
I will always have regard for your decrees.
118You reject all who stray from your decrees,
for their deceitfulness is in vain.
119All the wicked of the earth you discard like dross;
therefore I love your statutes.
120My flesh trembles in fear of you;
I stand in awe of your laws

121I have done what is righteous and just;
do not leave me to my oppressors.
122Ensure your servant's well-being;
let not the arrogant oppress me.
123My eyes fail, looking for your salvation,
looking for your righteous promise.
124Deal with your servant according to your love
and teach me your decrees.
125I am your servant; give me discernment
that I may understand your statutes.
126It is time for you to act, O LORD;
your law is being broken.
127Because I love your commands
more than gold, more than pure gold,
128and because I consider all your precepts right,
I hate every wrong path.

129Your statutes are wonderful;
therefore I obey them.
130The entrance of your words gives light;
it gives understanding to the simple.
131I open my mouth and pant,
longing for your commands.
132Turn to me and have mercy on me,
as you always do to those who love your name.
133Direct my footsteps according to your word;
let no sin rule over me.
134Redeem me from the oppression of men,
that I may obey your precepts.

135 Make your face shine upon your servant
and teach me your decrees.
136 Streams of tears flow from my eyes,
for your law is not obeyed.
137 Righteous are you, O LORD,
and your laws are right.
138 The statutes you have laid down are
righteous;
they are fully trustworthy.
139 My zeal wears me out,
for my enemies ignore your words.
140 Your promises have been thoroughly
tested,
and your servant loves them.
141 Though I am lowly and despised,
I do not forget your precepts.
142 Your righteousness is everlasting
and your law is true.
143 Trouble and distress have come upon me,
but your commands are my delight.
144 Your statutes are for ever right;
give me understanding that I may live.

145 I call with all my heart; answer me, O
LORD,
and I will obey your decrees.
146 I call out to you; save me
and I will keep your statutes.
147 I rise before dawn and cry for help;
I have put my hope in your word.
148 My eyes stay open through the watches
of the night,
that I may meditate on your promises.
149 Hear my voice in accordance with your
love;
renew my life, O LORD,
according to your laws.

150 Those who devise wicked schemes are near,
but they are far from your law.
151 Yet you are near, O LORD,
and all your commands are true.
152 Long ago I learned from your statutes
that you established them to last for ever.

153 Look upon my suffering and deliver me,
for I have not forgotten your law.
154 Defend my cause and redeem me;
renew my life according to your promise.
155 Salvation is far from the wicked,
for they do not seek out your decrees.
156 Your compassion is great, O LORD;
renew my life according to your laws.
157 Many are the foes who persecute me,
but I have not turned from your statutes.
158 I look on the faithless with loathing,
for they do not obey your word.
159 See how I love your precepts;
preserve my life, O LORD, according to your love.
160 All your words are true;
all your righteous laws are eternal.

161 Rulers persecute me without cause,
but my heart trembles at your word.
162 I rejoice in your promise
like one who finds great spoil.
163 I hate and abhor falsehood but I love your law.
164 Seven times a day I praise you
for your righteous laws.
165 Great peace have they who love your law,
and nothing can make them stumble.
166 I wait for your salvation, O LORD,
and I follow your commands.
167 I obey your statutes,
for I love then greatly –
168 I obey your precepts and your statutes,
169 May my cry come before you, O LORD;
give me understanding according to your word.
170 May my supplication come before you;
deliver me according to your promise.
171 May my lips overflow with praise,
for you teach me your decrees.
172 May my tongue sing of your word,
for all your commands are righteous.
173 May your hand be ready to help me,
for I have chosen your precepts.
174 I long for your salvation, O LORD,
and your law is my delight.
175 Let me live that I may praise you,
and may your laws sustain me.
176 I have strayed like a lost sheep.
Seek your servant,
for I have not forgotten your commandments.

The man who put the psalms together, some devout scholar of the Exile, divided his fifth book by a long psalm on the Word of God. He put it in the exact middle of the smaller collections out of which he built the book, perhaps for no other reason than that someone reading the 'Psalm of the Book' aloud would thus have an even weight in both hands as he unwound the roll.

He knew that, deprived of temple and ritual, the Word alone could hold the people together in the stress and temptations of a foreign land, and he put into an anthology, arranged alphabetically in sections of eight verses, one hundred and seventy-six sayings about the Word, either his own composition, or collected from one hundred and seventy-six fellow exiles.

It is possible to learn much about him. He longs for true happiness and knew that it lay only in goodness. That is why it was suggested that the same man wrote Psalm 1. Look at his first section and see the echo of Psalm 1 (1, 2). Happiness attached to steadfastness (4, 5), and a healthy awareness of temptation (5, 6), danger diminished only by remembering committal (7, 8) . . .

The third section (17-24) is peculiarly autobiographical. The writer had feared for his life (17), grieved over dryness of soul (18), known loneliness and rejection (19), stress (20), observed God's judgment (21); he claims reward for steadfastness (22), before powerful contempt (23), when none but God can guide (24) . . .

The 'whole heart' is his preoccupation (34, 58, 69, 145), the full obedience of the inner man. It was easy, as the exiles integrated, to forget Jerusalem, and settle

like Esther and Mordecai for the land of the conqueror. It was difficult not to waver under the enemy's persecution and contempt (22, 23, 61, 69), and faith had known what it was to stagger (31, 46). Opportunities awaited clever, adaptable Jews to make peace with Babylon or Susa (36, 37). There was grief in that thought (25, 28), and only safety in committal to the promises (10, 34, 58, 69, 145) . . . Perhaps we have, in this psalm, the beginnings of 'Pharisaism', when that word was a word of honour and signified the dedication of gifted scholars to holding fast the laws of God. We feel very close, in this psalm, to a great and good man, a man hidden in God, one of the fine founders of the synagogue system, which has always cemented a race together.

120 SLANDERED

I call on the LORD in my distress,
and he answers me.
2 Save me, O LORD, from lying lips
and from deceitful tongues.

3 What will he do to you, and what more
besides, O deceitful tongue?
4 He will punish you with a warrior's sharp
arrows,
with burning coals of the broom tree.

5 Woe to me that I dwell in Meshech,
that I live among the tents of Kedar!
6 Too long have I lived
among those who hate peace.
7 I am a man of peace;
but when I speak, they are for war.

A collection of fifteen psalms in this book is called 'Songs of Ascent'. The Greek Septuagint and the Latin Vulgate accepted the tradition that explained the name as a processional hymn sung by the Levites, going up the fifteen steps to the Court of the Men. Maybe 'songs of the goings-up', means 'pilgrim songs' as the returning exiles 'went up' to Jerusalem (Isaiah 30.29). The Jews still use the word 'aliyah' or 'ascent', for returning to Israel (Ezra 2.1). Every 'oleh' or 'one going up', by right has citizenship with all its obligations and privileges as soon as he sets foot on Israeli soil. With one exception, these hymns are short, a little plaintive, muted somewhat, as though conscious of the stern climb to home and nationhood.

This, the first in the group, is difficult to interpret, elusive in imagery, and best assigned to the tense days of Nehemiah, when slander burdened the hard-pressed Jews. Slander was dangerous under a jealous empire (2). The broom burned long and hot, like hatred (4). Verse 5 speaks of exile. Amid the world's alien evil, the Christian, too, can long at times, for 'the other shore'.

121 MY HELPER

I lift up my eyes to the hills–
where does my help come from?
2 My help comes from the LORD,
the Maker of heaven and earth.

3 He will not let your foot slip –
he who watches over you will not slumber;
4 indeed, he who watches over Israel
will neither slumber nor sleep.

5 The LORD watches over you –
the LORD is your shade at your right hand;
6 the sun will not harm you by day,
nor the moon by night.

7 The LORD will keep you from all harm –
he will watch over your life;
8 the LORD will watch over your coming and going
both now and for evermore.

Jerusalem is visible to the approaching pilgrim from almost any direction, a notched skyline on Judea's topmost ridge, the sacred goal of the exile's desire. God's 'keeping' has brought them to this blessed point, and the concept of God's sleepless watch is repeated six times in five verses.

The caravan is preparing to sleep (3, 4), and God stands sentry, like the friend in battle who covered the swordsman's exposed right side (5). Sun and moon signify two forms of danger, fierce and open in the day, mysterious and subtle in the night. God's care covers both (6). Indeed, it shields all the activities of life, begun, concluded, now and evermore (8).

This has always been a well-loved psalm. There is always a citadel above to which to look, always one to 'stand on my right hand' to guard life's bridges, one to whom our beginnings and our endings are a loving care.

122 JERUSALEM

I rejoiced with those who said to me,
'Let us go to the house of the LORD.'
2 Our feet are standing
in your gates, O Jerusalem.

3 Jerusalem is built like a city
that is closely compacted together.
4 That is where the tribes go up,
the tribes of the LORD,
to praise the name of the LORD
according to the statute given to Israel.
5 There the thrones for judgment stand,
the thrones of the house of David.

6 Pray for the peace of Jerusalem:
'May those who love you be secure.
7 May there be peace within your walls
and security within your citadels.'
8 For the sake of my brothers and friends,
I will say, 'Peace be within you.'
9 For the sake of the house of the LORD our God,
I will seek your prosperity.

Neither Septuagint nor Vulgate ascribe this psalm to David. If it was his as the title suggests, it must date from his later days, when Jerusalem was becoming a centre of religious pilgrimage.

God is not localised, but what Christian cannot sense the awe of standing in some place where the Lord stood? The writer had seen Jerusalem, hemmed between its ravines, crowded on its ridges, loaded even then with a millenium of history (3, 4).

Perhaps the last verses are a Levite addition. The word 'peace' is embedded in the city's name ('salem', 'shalom'), and it is sad irony that the 'holy city' has, from then till now, been a pivotal point of strife, a place of fearsome siege and hot contention.

123 HAVE MERCY . . .

I lift up my eyes to you,
to you whose throne is in heaven.
2 As the eyes of slaves look to the hand of their master,
as the eyes of a maid look to the hand of her mistress,
so our eyes look to the LORD our God,
till he shows us his mercy.
3 Have mercy on us, O LORD, have mercy on us,
for we have endured much contempt.
4 We have endured much ridicule from the proud,
much contempt from the arrogant.

A sad little hymn of one not yet liberated, looking intently for the movement of God's hand, as Nehemiah, functioning as the trusted cupbearer of the Persian monarch, must have watched, alert, as a trained servant would, for the movement of the royal hand.

The thought was habitual in the Jews of this time. The 'hand of God' was for them a sort of figure for 'God in action' (Ezra 7.6, 9, 28; and 8.18, 22, 31; Nehemiah 2.8, 18). In a strange land, as R.K. Harrison renders verse 3, the psalmist feels 'swamped with contempt', waiting, still in the darkness, prayer still unanswered. At such times it is only possible to 'lift up the eyes'. To allow them to rove on a lower level is to sense despair.

124 HELP IN DANGER

If the Lord had not been on our
side —
let Israel say —
[2]if the LORD had not been on our side
when men attacked us,
[3]when their anger flared against us,
they would have swallowed us alive;
[4]the flood would have engulfed us,
the torrent would have swept over us,
[5]the raging waters would have swept us
away.

[6]Praise be to the LORD,
who has not let us be torn by their teeth.
[7]We have escaped like a bird
out of the fowler's snare;
the snare has been broken,
and we have escaped.
[8]Our help is in the name of the LORD,
the Maker of heaven and earth.

The Septuagint and the Vulgate, those two most ancient versions of the Hebrew scriptures, do not mention David as author. There are Davidic echoes (Psalm 28.6; and 31.22), and it could be a Jew of the Restoration echoing an older psalm. It is of no significance.

The psalmist looks back in horror, as the mind sometimes does, at what might have been had not God intervened. A whole nation could have been swallowed like Korah (Numbers 16.32, 33), or swept away, like the debris on a valley floor when some cloudburst in the watershed fills the dry, sandy wadi cliff-high (Psalms 18.16; 69.1, 2; 144.7; Isaiah 8.7, 8; and 28.17; Matthew 7.27). The 'raging waters' (5) are a striking figure for arrogant imperialism. Or else evil was like a wild beast pouncing, or a fowler grasping a trapped and fluttering bird. The good sometimes feel thus threatened in an evil world—until they grasp 'the Lord and all he signifies' (that is 'the name of the Lord'—John 1.12).

125 UNSHAKEABLE

Those who trust in the LORD are
like Mount Zion,
which cannot be shaken but endures
for ever.
2 As the mountains surround Jerusalem,
so the LORD surrounds his people.
both now and for evermore.

3 The sceptre of the wicked will not remain
over the land allotted to the righteous,

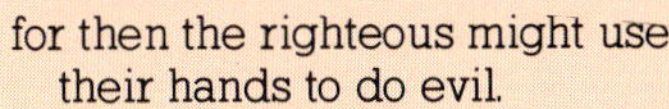

for then the righteous might use
their hands to do evil.

4 Do good, O LORD, to those who are good,
to those who are upright in heart.
5 But those who turn to crooked ways
the LORD will banish with the evildoers.

Peace be upon Israel.

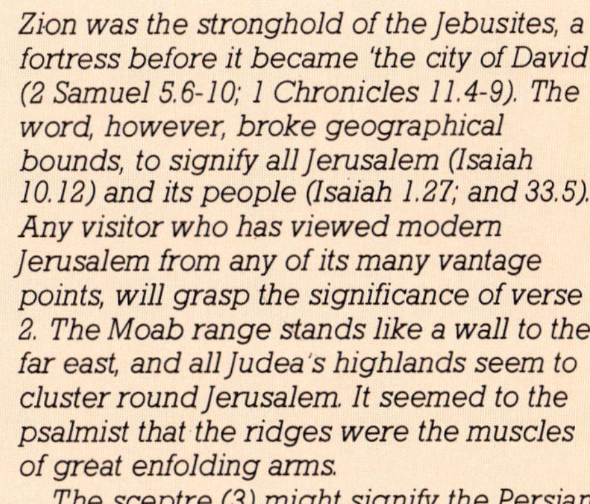

Zion was the stronghold of the Jebusites, a fortress before it became 'the city of David' (2 Samuel 5.6-10; 1 Chronicles 11.4-9). The word, however, broke geographical bounds, to signify all Jerusalem (Isaiah 10.12) and its people (Isaiah 1.27; and 33.5). Any visitor who has viewed modern Jerusalem from any of its many vantage points, will grasp the significance of verse 2. The Moab range stands like a wall to the far east, and all Judea's highlands seem to cluster round Jerusalem. It seemed to the psalmist that the ridges were the muscles of great enfolding arms.

The sceptre (3) might signify the Persian sceptre, for even restored Jerusalem was still part of the empire. The rest of these verses are obscure and may refer to obstruction from Susa provoked by the enemies who haunt the stories of Ezra and Nehemiah.

126 THE RETURN

When the LORD brought back
the captives to Zion,
we were like men who dreamed.
2Our mouths were filled with laughter,
our tongues with songs of joy.
Then it was said among the nations,
'The LORD has done great things for
them.'
3The LORD has done great things for us,
and we are filled with joy.

4Restore our fortunes, O LORD,
like streams in the Negev.
5Those who sow in tears
will reap with songs of joy.
6He who goes out weeping,
carrying seed to sow,
will return with songs of joy,
carrying sheaves with him.

Faithful exiles had kept alive the dream of Restoration, and now the reality breaks on an ecstatic pilgrim's view. There are moments in history and in life when some great dream comes true, some horror passes, a dawn breaks, 'when it is good to be alive' (1-3).

On such points of ecstasy there is no pausing. Hence the second group of three verses. The Negev ('the south') is an arid land, which can grow green only when the streams flow. So with the people. The tormented columns of captives had gone forth weeping to Babylon. There was a crop now to be reaped. The psalmist sees that the hard heart-searching of the dry and ravaged years could produce a crop of good. The winter was past. This psalm is one of the harvest sheaves.

127 CHILDREN

Unless the LORD builds the house,
its builders labour in vain.
Unless the LORD watches over the city,
the watchmen stand guard in vain.
2 In vain you rise early
and stay up late,
toiling for food to eat –
for he grants sleep to those he loves.

3 Sons are a heritage from the LORD,
children a reward from him.
4 Like arrows in the hands of a warrior
are sons born in one's youth.
5 Blessed is the man
whose quiver is full of them.
They will not be put to shame
when they contend with their enemies
in the gate.

Perhaps the traditional title of this psalm means 'by Solomon'. It is a fragment of 'wisdom literature', which could be from the wise king. It is not quite clear why it should be a 'song of ascent'. It pictures a settled society, not a pioneering one, and more in the atmosphere of Solomon's 'golden age' than of Jeremiah's beleaguered day.

A man of experience appears to reflect on life (1). Struggle and strife, the pain of ambition's pursuit, seem, as Ecclesiastes says, 'vanity', as he looks back (2). The blessings of a family are the chief boon of life (3). With a band of loyal sons, a man is like an archer with a quiver full of shafts . . .

It is a sad picture for our age, where the very family is under fire, abortion provokes horrifying debate, and childhood itself is unshielded from evil's most insidious assaults.

128 FRUITFULNESS

1 Blessed are all who fear the
LORD,
who walk in his ways.
2 You will eat the fruit of your labour;
blessings and prosperity will be yours.
3 Your wife will be like a fruitful vine
within your house;
your sons will be like olive shoots
round your table.
4 Thus is the man blessed
who fears the LORD.

5 May the LORD bless you from Zion
all the days of your life;
may you see the prosperity of Jerusalem,
6 and may you live to see your children's
children.

Peace be upon Israel.

If the last psalm, with its touch of 'wisdom literature', was the work of Solomon, so, surely, was this. It has a lighter touch than Psalm 127, and again pictures a more tranquil society than that suggested by the other 'songs of ascent'. The vine and the olive are familiar figures of fruitfulness and peace. We still offer 'the olive branch' for peace, for the olive, in ancient lands, was the first casualty of war, and the last to find restoration in anything less than a long tract of quietness.

Perhaps the writer, if not Solomon, was the compiler of the Psalter (see Psalm 1.1 and compare verse 1), who, at last turned to his land, and hoping for a 'patch of peace', wrote himself a marriage song. He feels that war is no longer near (Leviticus 26.6; Deuteronomy 28.30-33, 39, 40), home stable (2, 3), and his happiness assured, not only for his generation, but the next and the next (5, 6).

129 UNDEFEATED

They have greatly oppressed me from my youth –
let Israel say–
2 they have greatly oppressed me from my youth,
but they have not gained the victory over me.
3 Ploughmen have ploughed my back
and made their furrows long.
4 But the LORD is righteous;
he has cut me free from the cords of the wicked.

5 May all who hate Zion
be turned back in shame.
6 May they be like grass on the housetops,
which withers before it can grow;
7 with it the reaper cannot fill his hands,
nor the one who gathers fill his arms.
8 May those who pass by not say,
'The blessing of the LORD be upon you;
we bless you in the name of the LORD.'

The Captivity, for this psalmist, was still a memory of horror, conflict and persecution. And yet he has lived to see the righteousness of God vindicated. Israel, like the Church, has prevailed. 'The darkness has not overcome it' (John 1.5).

The psalmist was a countryman. Compare a townsman's image for the same humiliation (3; Isaiah 51.23). But the cord which tied the Jewish captive to the captor's plough, is cut by God (4).

Grass on the mud and straw roof, with no rootage or sustenance, withered at the first touch of drought (6). It was pulled up like weeds, a handful of rubbish (7). The last verse seems to reflect the 'shalom' of a passing wagon, and the happy greetings of some quiet harvest-time, as that shown in the little idyll of Ruth. It is a countryman's hymn. Perhaps many, in quiet corners, knew such quietness, even while Nehemiah struggled in tense Jerusalem. Ruth, after all, lived in the troubled days of the Judges.

130 OUT OF THE DEPTHS

Out of the depths I cry to you,
O LORD;
2 O Lord, hear my voice.
Let your ears be attentive
to my cry for mercy.

3 If you, O LORD, kept a record of sins,
O Lord, who could stand?
4 But with you there is forgiveness;
therefore you are feared.

5 I wait for the LORD, my soul waits,
and in his word I put my hope.
6 My soul waits for the Lord
more than watchmen wait for the
morning,
more than watchmen wait for the
morning.

7 O Israel, put your hope in the LORD,
for with the LORD is unfailing love
and with him is full redemption.
8 He himself will redeem Israel
from all their sins.

'A Pauline psalm', said Luther of this sixth and last of the 'penitential' psalms. The writer had sinned, and from the pit of agonised conviction, he cries aloud for help. 'If out of the depths we cry, we shall cry ourselves out of the depths' (Maclaren). Who, after all, does not need mercy (1-3)? And let those forgiven reverence the forgiver (4). The forgiveness is immediate and absolute, but that truth requires time to penetrate heart and brain. Assurance can be slow, as most sensitive souls who have known this experience realise (5, 6). 'Joy and gladness' are not a sudden sequence (Psalm 51.8, 12). But the next urge of the forgiven soul is the desire that others should know the blessing of his peace (7, 8; Psalm 51.13).

Oscar Wilde's agonising book 'De Profundis' takes its title from the Latin of the Vulgate version of the opening words. It is infinitely sad that the polished writer did not seem to reach the peace of the rest of the psalm.

131 HUMILITY

My heart is not proud, O LORD,
my eyes are not haughty;
I do not concern myself with great matters
or things too wonderful for me.
2 But I have stilled and quieted my soul;
like a weaned child with its mother,
like a weaned child is my soul within
me.

3 O Israel, put your hope in the LORD
both now and for evermore.

A fragment from the royal psalmist on the gentleness of the third Beatitude (Matthew 5.5). Humility is not a cringing, self-despising thing. It is quiet love. It is a sure test of greatness in learning, leadership, in any sphere of life. It is neither the greater man seeking to pass for the lesser, nor any conscious self-effacing at all. It is simple unselfconscious absence of pride and self-assertion. It never behaves unmannerly (1 Corinthians 13.5). It is quietness of soul (2).

The reader of this tiny psalm is overhearing a prayer to God, not boasting to men, for once humility is claimed it disappears. It is a small gem, which the compiler found, and for some reason stored here.

132 REMEMBER DAVID

O LORD, remember David
and all the hardships he endured.

2 He swore an oath to the LORD
and made a vow to the Mighty One of Jacob:
3 'I will not enter my house or go to my bed –
4 I will allow no sleep to my eyes,
no slumber to my eyelids,
5 till I find a place for the LORD,
a dwelling for the Mighty One of Jacob.'

6 We heard it in Ephrathah,
we came upon it in the fields of Jaar:
7 'Let us go to his swelling-place;
let us worship at his footstool –
8 arise, O LORD, and come to your resting place,
you and the ark of your might.
9 May your priests be clothed with righteousness;
may your saints sing for joy.'

10 For the sake of David your servant,
do not reject your anointed one.

11 The LORD swore an oath to David,
a sure oath that he will not revoke:
'One of your own descendants
I will place on your throne –
12 if your sons keep my covenant
and the statutes I teach them,
then their sons shall sit
on your throne for ever and ever.'

13 For the LORD has chosen Zion,
he has desired it for his dwelling:
14 'This is my resting place for ever and ever;
here I will sit enthroned, for I have desired it –
15 I will bless her with abundant provisions;
her poor will I satisfy with food.
16 I will clothe her priests with salvation,
and her saints shall ever sing for joy.

17 'Here I will make a horn grow for David
and set up a lamp for my anointed one.
18 I will clothe his enemies with shame,
but the crown on his head shall be resplendent.'

Possibly a song written for the housing of the Ark in Solomon's temple. Others conjecture the occasion of Psalm 24, or the consecration of the second temple under Zerubabbel. It is natural enough that David, whose unfulfilled desire the temple was, should be remembered (1). Such vows as those of verses 3 to 5 must be set in the context of Eastern hyperbole. David simply vowed that, amid all the activities of life, the providing of a suitable dwelling for the symbols of God's law should never be forgotten.

He had taken the first steps. Ephrathah is Bethlehem, David's home town (Genesis 35.16, 19; and 48.7; Ruth 4.11; Micah 5.2), and Jaar is Kirjath-jearim, the Ark's resting-place (1 Samuel 7.1, 2). Now at last the rich symbol can go to its fitting resting place (6-10), and for David's sake let

David's son be heir to the promise.

The clothing, of the final metaphor (18), is vivid. Apparel is the first visual impact of a person. Apply it to Augustine's verse—Romans 13.14.

The psalm was properly included among the psalms of pilgrimage because of its note of jubilation. It was a glad day.

133 BROTHERLY LOVE

How good and pleasant it is
when brothers live together in unity!
2 It is like precious oil poured on the head,
running down on the beard,
running down on Aaron's beard,
down upon the collar of his robes.
3 It is as if the dew of Hermon
were falling on Mount Zion.
For there the LORD bestows his blessing,
even life for evermore.

This small psalm could mark the time when at last the land was united under David as king. It was to be a full half-century of peace and unity, secure borders and tranquility. Underneath, discontent began to grow, as Absolom's rebellion was to indicate, and Solomon imposed burdens which ultimately, and only after his death, led to the division of the kingdom. But nothing marred the prospect when the guerrilla hero first held the throne. They were brothers, sons of a common father (1) . . .

The ancient world had no objection to oil on the garments, and the oil envisaged was scented with myrrh, and the symbol of the rich blessing of God (2). Hermon's snows are the source of the Jordan, which fills Galilee and the whole fruitful valley down to the Dead Sea. So, too, the rains and winter snows of the Judean uplands, precipitated by the west winds, whose eastern overflow gave the arid slopes of the western side of the Rift Valley any greenery they had. The mountain waters made the land one. So it was in this brief tract of calm. Unity can only exist among those who share a common source of good.

134 THE SANCTUARY

Praise the LORD, all you servants
of the LORD
who minister by night in the house of the
LORD.
2 Lift up your hands in the sanctuary
and praise the LORD.
3 May the LORD, the Maker of heaven and
earth,
bless you from Zion.

This piece is simply a benediction to close the series of pilgrim songs, and it was addressed to the priests, to be sung in greeting as the procession of worshippers entered the temple court.

135 GOD'S GREATNESS

Praise the LORD.

Praise the name of the LORD;
Praise him, you servants of the LORD,
2you who minister in the house of the LORD,
in the courts of the house of our God.

3Praise the LORD, for the LORD is good;
sing praise to his name, for that is pleasant.
4For the LORD has chosen Jacob to be his own,
Israel to be his treasured possession.

5I know that the LORD is great,
that our Lord is greater than all gods.
6The LORD does whatever pleases him,
in the heavens and on the earth,
in the seas and all their depths.
7He makes clouds rise from the ends of the earth;
he sends lightning with the rain
and brings out the wind from his storehouses.

8He struck down the firstborn of Egypt,
the firstborn of men and animals.
9He sent his signs and wonders into your midst, O Egypt,
against Pharaoh and all his servants.
10He struck down many nations
and killed mighty kings —
11Sihon king of the Amorites,
Og king of Bashan
and all the kings of Canaan —
12and he gave their land as an inheritance,
an inheritance to his people Israel.

13Your name, O LORD, endures for ever,
your renown, O LORD, through all generations.
14For the LORD will vindicate his people
and have compassion on his servants.

15The idols of the nations are silver and gold,
made by the hands of men.
16They have mouths, but cannot speak,
eyes, but they cannot see;
17they have ears, but cannot hear,
nor is there breath in their mouths.
18Those who make them will be like them,
and so will all who trust in them.

19O house of Israel, praise the LORD;
20O house of Levi, praise the LORD;
you who fear him, praise the LORD.
21Praise be to the LORD from Zion,
to him who dwells in Jerusalem.

Praise the LORD.

This and the next psalm are a small 'Hallel', or songs or praise, for some reason separated from the rest. The theme of both psalms is history, revealing God's majesty and his power over the brutal nations of the Middle East, and over the 'un-gods' they worshipped.

The first psalm is a poetic mosaic almost completely constructed out of fragments lifted from other psalms (nine of them), from Exodus (three), from Deuteronomy (two), from Job (one), Isaiah (one) and Jeremiah (two). The practice was common and laudable. Zephaniah echoes Jeremiah throughout. It also shows how well-known these passages were to the Jews of the Restoration, and how the traumatic experience of the nation's uprooting had driven them to the revealed Word, had for ever destroyed the once obsessive temptation to idolatry, and had made the Jews the 'people of the Book'.

136 HIS LOVE ENDURES

Give thanks to the LORD, for he is
good.
His love endures for ever.
2Give thanks to the God of gods.
His love endures for ever.
3Give thanks to the Lord of lords:
His love endures for ever.
4to him who alone does great wonders,
His love endures for ever.
5who by his understanding made the
heavens
His love endures for ever.
6who spread out the earth upon the waters,
His love endures for ever.
7who made the great lights —
His love endures for ever.
8the sun to govern the day,
His love endures for ever.
9the moon and stars to govern the night;
His love endures for ever.

10to him who struck down the firstborn of
Egypt
His love endures for ever.
11and brought Israel out from among them
His love endures for ever.
12with a mighty hand and outstretched arm;
His love endures for ever.

13to him who divided the Red Sea asunder
His love endures for ever.
14and brought Israel through the midst of it,
His love endures for ever.
15but swept Pharaoh and his army into the
Red Sea;
His love endures for ever.

16to him who led his people through the
desert,
His love endures for ever.
17who struck down great kings,
His love endures for ever
18and killed mighty kings —
His love endures for ever.
19Sihon king of the Amorites
His love endures for ever.
20and Og king of Bashan —
His love endures for ever.
21and gave their land as an inheritance,
His love endures for ever.
22an inheritance to his servant Israel;
His love endures for ever
23to the One who remembered us in our
low estate
His love endures for ever.
24and freed us from our enemies,
His love endures for ever.
25and who gives food to every creature.
His love endures for ever.

26Give thanks to the God of heaven.
His love endures for ever.

The psalm practically repeats its predecessor adding only, for choric or liturgical purposes, a refrain, which turns it into a chant. It again demonstrates the blessedness of retreat into the past, and the worship of praise. In Psalm 136, the emphasis shifts from praise to gratitude. Between the two there is small distinction.

The word 'kindness' is the closest English can get to the Hebrew 'chesedh' of the refrain. Perhaps the beautiful 'loving kindness' is best. The RSV's 'steadfast love' is close, but 'covenant love' of some translations is remote, and 'love' here not full enough.

137 EXILE

By the rivers of Babylon we sat
and wept
when we remembered Zion.
2There on the poplars we hung our harps,
3for there our captors asked us for songs,
our tormentors demanded songs of joy;
they said, 'Sing us one of the songs of
Zion!'

4How can we sing the songs of the LORD
while in a foreign land?
5If I forget you, O Jerusalem,
may my right hand forget its skill.
6May my tongue cling to the roof of my
mouth
if I do not remember you,
if I do not consider Jerusalem my highest
joy.

7Remember, O LORD, what the Edomites
did
on the day Jerusalem fell.
'Tear it down,' they cried,
'tear it down to its foundations!'

8O Daughter of Babylon, doomed to
destruction,
happy is he who repays you
for what you have done to us —
9he who seizes your infants
and dashes them against the rocks.

This psalm beginning beautifully and sadly, and its abrupt change at verse 7 into a shocking 'commination', or curse, has puzzled many. It makes sense if it is a dramatic recollection of a moment of peril.

When they had no synagogue, the Jews met by a river (Acts 16.13). A little group has been singing quietly by the willow-lined Euphrates, when a hostile crowd gathers, and demands a performance. It was dire danger on the edge of the great river and the only defence the menaced group had was to sing a 'song of cursing' (7-9).

They turn and invoke on Babylon what they had seen the brutal soldiers of Nebuchadnezzar inflict on them. The ancient (and modern) East, takes such solemn commination seriously. A formal curse was a potent weapon, whose words could haunt, madden and destroy. It was the Jews' last resort, and evidently sent the horrified persecutors away, for this writer survived, and remembered the awful incident.

In Christ, such weapons fell from the hands, but the curse must have still been practised, or Paul would not have deprecated it (Romans 12.14).

138 GOD'S CARE

I will praise you, O LORD, with
all my heart;
before the 'gods' I will sing your praise.
2 I will bow down towards your holy temple
and will praise your name
for your love and your faithfulness,
for you have exalted above all things
your name and your word.
3 When I called, you answered me;
you made me bold and stout-hearted.

4 May all the kings of the earth praise you, O
LORD,
when they hear the words of your mouth.
5 May they sing of the ways of the LORD,
for the glory of the LORD is great.

6 Though the LORD is on high, he looks upon
the lowly,
but the proud he knows from afar.
7 Though I walk in the midst of trouble,
you preserve my life;
you stretch out your hand against the anger
of my foes,
with your right hand you save me.
8 The LORD will fulfil his purpose for me;
your love, O LORD, endures for ever —
do not abandon the works of your hands.

The Septuagint offers Haggai and Zephaniah as rival authors. David is more likely, for all this final group of his psalms bear the imprint of his spirit, strain and testing, temptation, as well as gladness. Perhaps the group of Davidic hymns came late into the compiler's hands, or else he wished, amid the formalities of Book Five, to turn back before the final songs of praise to the songs of the earlier Psalter.

The opening verse is not meant to give substance to the heathens' gods, haunting though the Hebrews found the thought of them in times of suffering, until the Exile purged their minds for ever. The old evangelistic note slips again into verse 4, with a world praising God (5), a God inaccessible only to the proud (6). It was a psalm worth revival at the Restoration. The 'valley' was passed (7).

139 GOD'S PRESENCE

O LORD, you have searched me,
and you know me.
2You know when I sit and when I rise;
you perceive my thoughts from afar.
3You discern my going out and my lying
down;
you are familiar with all my ways.
4Before a word is on my tongue
you know it completely, O LORD.

5You hem me in, behind and before;
you have laid your hand upon me.
6Such knowledge is too wonderful for me,
too lofty for me to attain.

7Where can I go from your Spirit?
Where can I flee from your presence?
8If I go up to the heavens, you are there;
if I make my bed in the depths, you are
there.
9If I rise on the wings of the dawn,
if I settle on the far side of the sea,
10even there your hand will guide me,
your right hand will hold me fast.

11If I say, 'Surely the darkness will hide me
and the light become night around me,'
12even the darkness will not be dark to you;
the night will shine like the day,
for darkness is a light to you.

13For you created my inmost being;
you knit me together in my mother's
womb.
14I praise you because I am fearfully and
wonderfully made;
your works are wonderful,
I know that full well.
15My frame was not hidden from you
when I was made in the secret place.
When I was woven together in the depths
of the earth,
16 your eyes saw my unformed body.
All the days ordained for me
were written in your book
before one of them came to be.

17How precious to me are your thoughts, O
God!
How vast is the sum of them!
18Were I to count them,
they would outnumber the grains of
sand.
When I awake,
I am still with you.

19If only you would slay the wicked, O God!
Away from me, you bloodthirsty men!
20They speak of you with evil intent;
your adversaries misuse your name.
21Do I not hate those who hate you, O LORD,
and abhor those who rise up against
you?
22I have nothing but hatred for them;
I count them my enemies.

23Search me, O God, and know my heart;
test me and know my anxious thoughts.
24See if there is any offensive way in me,
and lead me in the way everlasting.

With passing years, and a lengthening tract of life behind, many become conscious of the pursuit, the almost relentless pursuit of God, and his unabated pressure to penetrate all life, and bring it to complete surrender. It is folly to resist or oppose such love (1-10).

It is a thought to remember in the darkness that the Pursuer is always there (11, 12). He has followed since earliest days (13-16), as many, who reflect on much which might have been, realise with awe. Wonder, said Plato, is the beginning of all philosophy. It can also be the foundation of worship (17, 18).

How revolting is evil and arrogance before such a thought (19-22)! The words are strong, but the psalmist merely signifies his utter surrender to God. To offer the open heart to such scrutiny as verses 23 and 24 invite is brave, but it should be dared in the light of John 3.19-21. Dare we?

140 LIKE SERPENT'S TONGUES

1Rescue me, O LORD, from evil
men;
protect me from men of violence,
2who devise evil plans in their hearts
and stir up war every day.
3They make their tongues as sharp as a
serpent's;
the poison of vipers is on their
lips. *Selah*

4Keep me, O LORD, from the hands of the
wicked;
protect me from men of violence
who plan to trip my feet.
5Proud men have hidden a snare for me;
they have spread out the cords of their
net
and have set traps for me along my
path. *Selah*

[6]O LORD, I say to you, 'You are my God.
Hear, O LORD, my cry for mercy.
[7]O Sovereign LORD, my strong deliverer,
who shields my head in the day of
battle –
[8]do not grant the wicked their desires, O
LORD;
do not let their plans succeed,
or they will become proud. *Selah*

[9]Let the heads of those who surround me
be covered with the trouble their lips
have caused.
[10]Let burning coals fall upon them;
may they be thrown into the fire,
into miry pits, never to rise.
[11]Let slanderers not be established in the
land;
may disaster hunt down men of violence.

[12]I know that the LORD secures justice for
the poor
and upholds the cause of the needy.
[13]Surely the righteous will praise your
name
and the upright will live before you.

A loathing of violence, slander and treachery find their way into many of David's psalms of which this is one. If these psalms were those especially relevant in the menaced days of the Restoration, how truly are they relevant now in a violence-ridden world (1, 2).

Along with deliberately plotted violence (2), goes the coward's weapon of slander (3), the stock-in-trade of the arrogant and the hater of the good (5). The only weapon against such evil is prayer, the only helmet God's shadowing hand (6, 7). There is nothing wrong with the fervent prayer which follows (8-11). To seek the end of evil is not an unworthy sentiment. Evil is self-destructive, its defeat is inbuilt, and in the end good must prevail.

141 A PRAYER

¹O LORD, I call to you; come quickly
to me.
Hear my voice when I call to you.
²May my prayer be set before you like
incense;
may the lifting up of my hands be like
the evening sacrifice.

³Set a guard over my mouth, O LORD;
keep watch over the door of my lips.
⁴Let not my heart be drawn to what is evil,
to take part in wicked deeds
with men who are evildoers;
let me not eat of their delicacies.

⁵Let a righteous man strike me – it is a
kindness;
let him rebuke me – it is oil on my head.
My head will not refuse it.

Yet my prayer is ever against the deeds of
evildoers;
⁶ their rulers will be thrown down from the
cliffs,
and the wicked will learn that my words
were well spoken.
⁷They will say, 'As one ploughs and breaks
up the earth,
so our bones have been scattered at the
mouth of the grave.'

⁸But my eyes are fixed on you, O Sovereign
LORD;
in you I take refuge – do not give me
over to death.
⁹Keep me from the snares they have laid
for me,
from the traps set by evildoers.
¹⁰Let the wicked fall into their own nets,
while I pass by in safety.

Denied access to formal worship, in one of his retreats to the protecting wilderness, David begs that the lifting of his hands may suffice for incense and sacrifice (1-2). He knew where evil begins, in a word, and in the corruption which inspires the word (Psalm 51.6, 10; Luke 6.45). Association with evil men can corrupt, as Lewis so vividly describes in his perceptive essay 'The Inner Ring' (3, 4). Just reproach David will accept (5), and is sure, that evil-doers will come to justice (6).

Some ancient textual difficulties impose a task on translators of the last four verses, but the sequence of thought is familiar, the suicidal nature of evil, vindication for the wronged, and the apocalyptic ruin of the wicked. In such trust, the psalmist looks up.

142 SET ME FREE

I cry aloud to the LORD;
  I lift up my voice to the LORD for mercy.
2 I pour out my complaint before him;
  before him I tell my trouble.

3 When my spirit grows faint within me,
  it is you who know my way.
In the path where I walk
  men have hidden a snare for me.
4 Look to my right and see;
  no one is concerned for me.
I have no refuge;
  no one cares for my life.

5 I cry to you, O LORD;
  I say, 'You are my refuge,
  my portion in the land of the living.'
6 Listen to my cry,
  for I am in desperate need;
rescue me from those who pursue me,
  for they are too strong for me.
7 Set me free from my prison
  that I may praise your name.
Then the righteous will gather about me
  because of your goodness to me.

It is a time of grief and trouble, perhaps the days of Psalm 57, but the mood lacks the jubilation of the earlier psalm. There is only one place to 'empty out grief', as R.K. Harrison renders verse 2. He does that, and in the darkness he can do no more (3).

But there seems a Presence on the path of snares, even when all the rest, even his sword-arm companion, have gone. The pursuit ('pursuer' and 'persecutor' of variant translations, are, after all, the same word) is hot behind, noisy, near (5,6). He feels trapped, imprisoned, and longs for the protecting wall of his friends (7).

An experience, no doubt, from guerrilla days, but now close to the strife of life. These are real words to use when we feel hemmed in, claustrophobic, darkly lonely, exposed to evil . . .

143 TROUBLE

O LORD, hear my prayer,
listen to my cry for mercy;
in your faithfulness and righteousness
come to my relief.
2 Do not bring your servant into judgment,
for no one living is righteous before you.

3 The enemy pursues me,
he crushes me to the ground;
he makes me dwell in darkness
like those long dead.
4 So my spirit grows faint within me;
my heart within me is dismayed.

5 I remember the days of long ago;
I meditate on all your works
and consider what your hands have
done.
6 I spread out my hands to you;
my soul thirsts for you like a parched
land. *Selah*

7 Answer me quickly, O LORD;
my spirit faints with longing.
Do not hide your face from me
or I will be like those who go down to
the pit.
8 Let the morning bring me word of your
unfailing love,
for I have put my trust in you.
Show me the way I should go,
for to you I lift up my soul.
9 Rescue me from my enemies, O LORD,
for I hide myself in you.
10 Teach me to do your will,
for you are my God;
may your good Spirit
lead me on level ground.

11 For your name's sake, O LORD, preserve
my life;
in your righteousness, bring me out of
trouble.
12 In your unfailing love, silence my
enemies;
destroy all my foes,
for I am your servant.

This psalm, a companion-piece, perhaps, to Psalm 51, is the last of the 'penitential' psalms.

God's faithfulness and righteousness are the basis of the plea (1). He is 'faithful and just (note the word) and will forgive . . .' (1 John 1.9). It is 'mercy all', or no man is justified. Verses 3 and 4 are loaded with pain. In moments of our deepest

conviction, the Enemy presses hard. It is awesome to know that Christ must have known such assaults (Hebrews 4.15, 16). 'His love in times past . . .' can be a refuge. Like a drought-baked desert, the psalmist longs for the refreshment of the life-giving rain (6).

The last six verses become a tissue of quotations. In the agony of his mind, the penitent cannot find his own words. Scripture, well remembered, supplies them.

It is a psalm for those days of God's seeming withdrawal, when heaven seems of brass, and when the child of God, seemingly abandoned, continues to obey. If he cries: 'Why have you forsaken me?'—after all, he is quoting Christ.

144 GOD'S RULE

[1]Praise be to the LORD, my Rock,
who trains my hands for war,
my fingers for battle.
[2]He is my loving God and my fortress,
my stronghold and my deliverer,
my shield, in whom I take refuge,
who subdues peoples under me.

[3]O LORD, what is man that you care for him,
the son of man that you think of him?
[4]Man is like a breath;
his days are like a fleeting shadow.

[5]Part your heavens, O LORD, and come
down;
touch the mountains, so that they smoke.
[6]Send forth lightning and scatter the
enemies;
shoot your arrows and rout them.
[7]Reach down your hand from on high;
deliver me and rescue me
from the mighty waters,
from the hands of foreigners
[8]whose mouths are full of lies,
whose right hands are deceitful.

[9]I will sing a new song to you, O God;
on the ten-stringed lyre I will make
music to you,
[10]to the One who gives victory to kings,
who delivers his servant David from the
deadly sword.

[11]Deliver me and rescue me
from the hands of foreigners
whose mouths are full of lies,
whose right hands are deceitful.

[12]Then our sons in their youth
will be like well-nurtured plants,
and our daughters will be like pillars
carved to adorn a palace.
[13]Our barns will be filled
with every kind of provision.
Our sheep will increase by thousands,
by tens of thousands in our fields;
[14]our oxen will draw heavy loads.
There will be no breaching of walls,
no going into captivity,
no cry of distress in our streets.

[15]Blessed are the people of whom this is
true;
blessed are the people whose God is
the LORD.

This is another Davidic anthology, either the author's own making, or the compilers', setting out an arrangement for liturgical use.

The pattern is ordered thus: the collection begins with storm and danger and merges more quietly into prayer. The prayer finds consummation in a land at peace. The good man's sons are like green trees, his daughters, like 'pillars carved to adorn a palace' (12)—like Athens' lovely caryatides supporting the porch of the Erechtheum. Pause on the rendering of the last part of verse 14, as Harrison renders it: '. . . that there be no disturbances in our city streets.'

145 GOD'S WONDERS

I will exalt you, my God the King;
I will praise your name for ever and ever.
[2]Every day I will praise you
and extol your name for ever and ever.

[3]Great is the LORD and most worthy of praise;
his greatness no one can fathom.
One generation will commend your works to another;
they will tell of your mighty acts.
[5]They will speak of the glorious splendour of your majesty,
and I will meditate on your wonderful works.
[6]They will tell of the power of your awesome works,
and I will proclaim your great deeds.
[7]They will celebrate your abundant goodness
and joyfully sing of your righteousness.

[8]The LORD is gracious and compassionate,
slow to anger and rich in love.
[9]The LORD is good to all;
he has compassion on all he has made.
[10]All you have made will praise you, O LORD;
your saints will extol you.
[11]They will tell of the glory of your kingdom
and speak of your might,
[12]so that all men may know of your mighty acts
and the glorious splendour of your kingdom.
[13]Your kingdom is an everlasting kingdom,
and your dominion endures through all generations.

The LORD is faithful to all his promises
and loving towards all he has made.
[14]The LORD upholds all those who fall
and lifts up all who are bowed down.
[15]The eyes of all look to you,
and you give them their food at the proper time.
[16]You open your hand
and satisfy the desires of every living thing.

[17]The LORD is righteous in all his ways
and loving towards all he has made.
[18]The LORD is near to all who call on him,
to all who call on him in truth.
[19]He fulfils the desires of those who fear him;
he hears their cry and saves them.
[20]The LORD watches over all who love him,
but all the wicked he will destroy.

[21]My mouth will speak in praise of the LORD.
Let every creature praise his holy name
for ever and ever.

The last of the group of David's psalms, and the last of the alphabetical psalms, until a Qumran cave supplied the missing fragment opening with 'nun' ('n').

David's insight grasped how little man's mind can comprehend of God. It is the Christian's privilege to know God in human terms, 'made flesh'. God, nevertheless, reveals himself in history, majestic, righteous, and sometimes 'terrible' (4-7). 'Grace and truth' were only revealed in Christ (John 1.14). That is why verses 8 and 9 demonstrate such leaps of understanding . . .

The preoccupation of Book Five of the Psalter is God in creation and in history (10-12). In the great school of world events the Jews learned the fragility of empires (13). The ruler's true glory is not to ride laurelled 'to lap the fat of the years', but to lift the fallen, feed the multitude and bless the common man (14-16). God is such a ruler, available (18), just to all (19), inexorable towards evil (20) . . . And so the doxology of a great poet (21), a sensitive man, a sinner saved by grace, who reached high, fell low, knew God and God's forgiveness.

146 GOD'S CHARACTER

Praise the LORD.

Praise the LORD, O my soul.
2 I will praise the LORD all my life;
I will sing praise to my God as long as I live.

3 Do not put your trust in princes,
in mortal men, who cannot save.
4 When their spirit departs, they return to the ground;
on that very day their plans come to nothing.

5 Blessed is he whose help is the God of Jacob,
whose hope is in the LORD his God,
6 the Maker of heaven and earth,
the sea, and everything in them—
the LORD, who remains faithful for ever.
7 He upholds the cause of the oppressed
and gives food to the hungry.
The LORD sets prisoners free,
8 the LORD gives sight to the blind,
the LORD lifts up those who are bowed down,
the LORD loves the righteous.
9 The LORD watches over the alien
and sustains the fatherless and the widow,
but he frustrates the ways of the wicked.

10 The LORD reigns for ever,
your God, O Zion, for all generations.

Praise the LORD.

In the Septuagint this small hymn is ascribed to Haggai and Zechariah. Haggai was called to urge a weary people to finish the temple whose building lagged. It was 520 BC. Zechariah's burden was to bring a careless people to more devoted worship in the finished shrine.

Such tasks are a heavy load, and, if either prophet wrote this psalm, it is stirring to find in it no word of complaining. He chose praise to give to those whose hands were weary, and whose hearts grew cold. Man, at such times, is not a staff to lean upon (3, 4). In the Psalms' last Beatitude, everything the writer knows of God, echoes to the music beat round the still ruined city.

147 FAITHFUL FOR EVER

Praise the LORD

How good it is to sing praises to our God,
how pleasant and fitting to praise him!

2 The LORD builds up Jerusalem;
he gathers the exiles of Israel.
3 He heals the broken-hearted
and binds up their wounds.

4 He determines the number of the stars
and calls them each by name.
5 Great is our Lord and mighty in power;
his understanding has no limit.
6 The LORD sustains the humble
but casts the wicked to the ground.

7 Sing to the LORD with thanksgiving;
make music to our God on the harp.
8 He covers the sky with clouds;
he supplies the earth with rain
and makes grass grow on the hills.
9 He provides food for the cattle
and for the young ravens when they call.

10 His pleasure is not in the strength of the
horse,
nor his delight in the legs of a man;
11 the LORD delights in those who fear him,
who put their hope in his unfailing love.

12 Extol the LORD, O Jerusalem;
praise your God, O Zion,
13 for he strengthens the bars of your gates
and blesses your people within you.
14 He grants peace to your borders
and satisfies you with the finest of wheat.

15 He sends his command to the earth;
his word runs swiftly.
16 He spreads the snow like wool
and scatters the frost like ashes.
17 He hurls down his hail like pebbles.
Who can withstand his icy blast?
18 He sends his word and melts them;
he stirs up his breezes, and the waters
flow.

19 He has revealed his word to Jacob,
his laws and decrees to Israel.
20 He has done this for no other nation;
they do not know his laws.

Praise the LORD.

A psalm, perhaps from Nehemiah's brave days when, from the presence of his king he had brought encouragement to the remnant of exiled Judah, who had chosen to go back to the tumbled ruin of Jerusalem and build the nation's life again.

The pioneers were broken by discouragement. They were unwalled and exposed to their enemies in a humiliation which Nehemiah's memoir describes. And now the walls were growing again (2, 12, 13).

There were those who in zeal had left loved ones in exile, and with adversity chilling endeavour, grieved and doubted (3-5). Let them look at history. Dread Babylon was down (6); they lived. And the stony hills, so long untilled, were green and watered (8, 9). Even the dark raven was heard and fed, much more, surely God's people (9). Strife on the borderlands was dying (14). Like the swift Persian post, God's commandments went out. He, not long forgotten Baal, was Lord of wind and weather. 'Simply look upwards and trust him the more . . .'

148 GREAT IS OUR LORD

Praise the LORD.

Praise the LORD from the heavens,
praise him in the heights above.
2 Praise him, all his angels,
praise him, all his heavenly hosts.
3 Praise him, sun and moon,
praise him, all you shining stars.
4 Praise him, you highest heavens
and you waters above the skies.
5 Let them praise the name of the LORD,
for he commanded and they were created.
6 He set them in place for ever and ever;
he gave a decree that will never pass away.

7 Praise the LORD from the earth,
you great sea creatures and all ocean depths,
8 lightning and hail, snow and clouds,
stormy winds that do his bidding,
9 you mountains and all hills,
fruit trees and all cedars,
10 wild animals and all cattle,
small creatures and flying birds,
11 kings of the earth and all nations,
you princes and all rulers on earth,
12 young men and maidens,
old men and children.

13 Let them praise the name of the LORD,
for his name alone is exalted;
his splendour is above the earth and the heavens.
14 He has raised up for his people a horn,
the praise of all his saints,
of Israel, the people close to his heart.

Praise the LORD.

Israel is a varied land, geologically and geographically full of contrast in scenery. It is rich in surprises in vista and colour. Trampled and ravaged by war, burned and devastated through the ages, its soil forgives the spoiler, responds to the care enjoined on Adam, put in a garden—the Hebrew literally says 'to serve it' (Genesis 2.15) . . . Populations were torn from it to fill the empty lands of empires or to toil in servitude. Assyria, Babylon, Rome all harmed and emptied the land. And now the psalmist sees a full countryside again, God's laws obeyed in the ordered heavens, in the permanence of landscape, the strength of the hills, the rejuvenating forests, the teeming cattle and the growing population.

One senses again and again in these closing psalms the warmth of that morning of history when the exiles, or those who would, came home. Was it Ezra who wrote them, or some other who, like him, felt it was a dawn in which it was good to be alive, and 'to be young was very heaven'? God send a weary world such days, and grant the new Israel such exultation.

149 LET ISRAEL REJOICE

Praise the LORD.

Sing to the LORD a new song,
his praise in the assembly of the saints.

2Let Israel rejoice in their Maker;
let the people of Zion be glad in their King.
3Let them praise his name with dancing
and make music to him with tambourine and harp.
4For the LORD takes delight in his people;
he crowns the humble with salvation.
5Let the saints rejoice in this honour
and sing for joy on their beds.

6May the praise of God be in their mouths
and a double-edged sword in their hands,
7to inflict vengeance on the nations
and punishment on the peoples,
8to bind their kings with fetters,
their nobles with shackles of iron,
9to carry out the sentence written against them.
This is the glory of all his saints.

Praise the LORD.

Nehemiah movingly describes his valiant 'few' at work with swords unsheathed (6; Nehemiah 4.17). This ringing song of victory may date from that occasion. The verve and 'gusto', to use C.S. Lewis' word for some Jewish praise, is necessarily more tempered and quietly reverential for the Christian who lives on the other side of a cross and a grave, and knows what it cost God to bring man salvation. To the psalmist God was the great Redeemer who bent history and circumstance to his people's blessing. Christian worship begins with the blood of Christ and the awesome thought of God in Christ 'reconciling the world to himself'. We have more for adoration than a newly-walled Jerusalem (1-3).

'Beds' (5) can be literal. There is no need to make it prayer mats (NEB). There are times when to sleep unharmed and unafraid is benediction. Then the triumphant little song becomes something like America's 'battle hymn'. Their eyes 'have seen the glory of the coming of the Lord'. The land is alive again, destiny resumes, hostile hands have been dashed aside, and 'his day is marching on'. It is good to thank God for being part of a mighty enterprise. We are.

150 MAKE MUSIC

Praise the LORD.

Praise God in his sanctuary;
  praise him in his mighty heavens.
2 Praise him for his acts of power;
  praise him for his surpassing greatness.
3 Praise him with the sounding of the trumpet,
  praise him with the harp and lyre,
4 praise him with tambourine and dancing,
  praise him with the strings and flute,
5 praise him with the clash of cymbals,
  praise him with resounding cymbals.

6 Let everything that has breath praise the LORD.

Praise the LORD.

The final psalm in the Psalter, like the first, is probably the work of the compiler of the whole collection. It could be no other than a benediction of praise, as the conclusion of any great work of God must be. The writer calls on every imaginable instrument of praise to join and orchestrate his hallelujah.

If, indeed, the psalm before this dated from the middle of the fifth century before Christ, and Moses had an earlier portion in the song-book of the second temple, the rabbi who, in exile perhaps, put the whole collection together, had lived in awed imagination through eight centuries of his people's praise and pain and prayer. He had heard the voices of king and prophet, of poet and preacher, of victory, defeat, perplexity and adoration. He had journeyed through all history, as men feel and suffer history, ride its billows or roll beneath them. Such is the theme of the Bible.